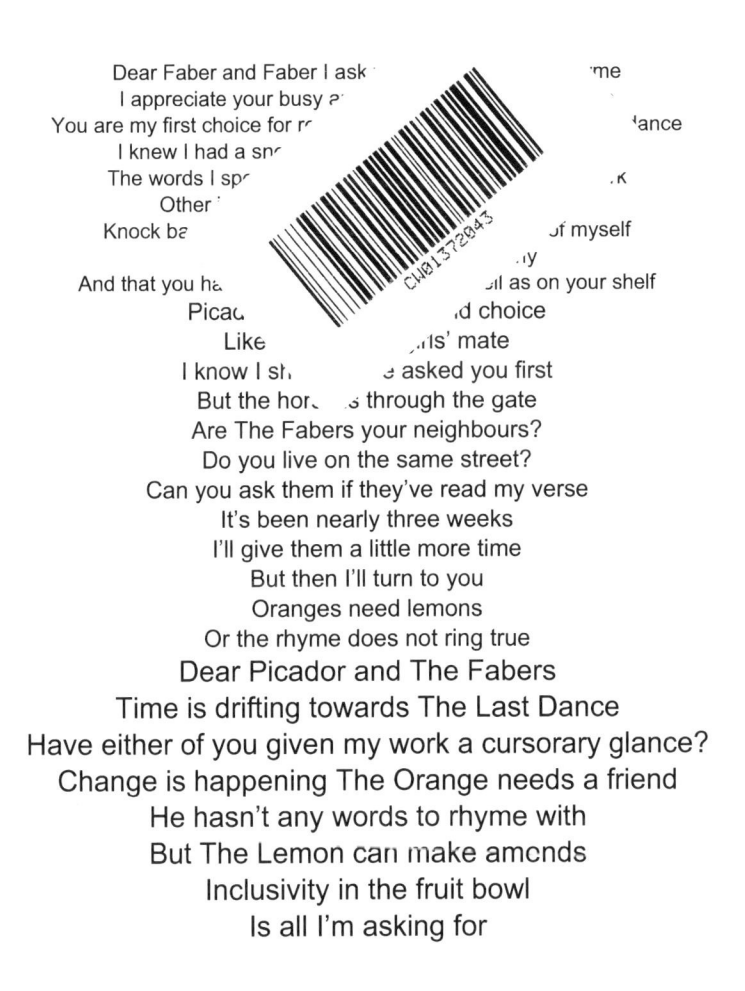

Dear Faber and Faber I ask ⁓me
I appreciate your busy ?⁓
You are my first choice for r⁓ ⁓ance
I knew I had a sn⁓
The words I sp⁓ ⁓⁓
Other ⁓
Knock b⁓ ⁓f myself
⁓y
And that you h⁓ ⁓l as on your shelf
Pica⁓ ⁓d choice
Lik⁓ ⁓ıs' mate
I know I s⁓ ⁓ asked you first
But the ho⁓ ⁓ through the gate
Are The Fabers your neighbours?
Do you live on the same street?
Can you ask them if they've read my verse
It's been nearly three weeks
I'll give them a little more time
But then I'll turn to you
Oranges need lemons
Or the rhyme does not ring true
Dear Picador and The Fabers
Time is drifting towards The Last Dance
Have either of you given my work a cursorary glance?
Change is happening The Orange needs a friend
He hasn't any words to rhyme with
But The Lemon can make amends
Inclusivity in the fruit bowl
Is all I'm asking for

I love my poems.
Collectively they are as good as any.
In my opinion.
If you choose to read them you may form another
which may well hold value and merit.
It will not affect my own as I know my assertion is correct.
Opinions that I care for are from those I care for.
Humanity's destructive folly since the fanciful Garden Of Eden.

In my opinion.

For Kitkat
Alex and Lily

Special thanks to Mrs Rita Poole
for inclusion of her delightful prose.
Carys and Alan: The Alternative Lyricists

Don't be so selfish

What do you mean you've just had a baby
What do you mean money's hard to find
What do you mean you've had a bereavement
What do you mean poetry's the last thing on your mind
What do you mean you're on a course of chemotherapy
What do you mean you're going through a divorce
What do you mean you've lost your phone
What do you mean the Wi-fi's down

Don't be so selfish and self-absorbed
I'm only asking you to buy my book and read my rhyme

Oh you have……Thanks very much

**MEMORY HAS A BIAS NOT ALWAYS SINCERE
AND TIME IS A THIEF THAT WILL HIJACK THE TRUTH**

THE LEMON

Suck me! squeeze me!
I don't want you to share me
I'm bitter and refreshing
And I won't (taste of pith)

SLOTH PIGRIZIA

CONTENTS:

THE LEMON
GRAVESIDE
THE QUESTION OF INCLUSIVITY
ARCHWAY STATION
TERRY HANS CHRISTIAN
SUMMERTREES ROAD
MOFFF-EATEN PICASSO
THE MEDIUM
SCHRODINGERS DOG
MATTHEW STREET: A DAY IN ITS LIFE
SHAMEFUL TOURIST
KATE: THE RAREST EGG
WOMEN I SALUTE YOU
IRELAND THROUGH THE LENS OF A TEN-YEAR-OLDS EYE
JESUS WEPT WITH WOLSTENHOLME
FOCUS EARLY DOORS
JUDGEMENT
SENTINEL de la BODEGAS
ALADINS CAVE: RON AND MICHAEL
INFLUENTIAL FLOW
OBAN
ALEX
REDEMPTIVE ROAD
I.K.BRUNEL
GOOD JOB ALEX B
COMMENTATORS GLOSSARY
CONSPIRACY
THE ODD THE BAD OUTWEIGH THE LOVELY
PARLEZMEANINGLESSHOTAIREANS
DON BRADMAN
GLASGOW 1.30AM
GRANDDAUGHTER
RITA JACQUES
MEMOIRS OF RITA JACQUES
IT'S GETTING BETTER?
THE RED ONE OVERSEEING ALBAICIN
VIENNA MEANS NOTHING TO ME EXCEPT RISING DAMP
STANLOW
SUFFIX ON SUFFERANCE
FARANTOIREACHTA CARRAIG
THE HUMAN NATURE OF BIRDS
ARROGANCE
NIGEL: A CUT ABOVE
WILLIAM ERNEST

Graveside

Sodden cloth and sodden clod
The robin genuflects to God
Numbness clogs the monologue
Dank dampness mists the air and eyes
Umbrellas drip black gloved to hold
Despair to shelter in the fold
Uneasy fits the mourning suit
Tied throats restrict the Adam's fruit
Emotion peeling its manly skin
Wells of eyes belie within
I rest not easy in my mind
Thoughts alone and so confined
Grief singular serene
Its bitterness intensely sweet
I see the end I see the born
Aloof in thought deep trenchant yet
Treasured pain restrained to share
I search for you alas not there

The Question of Inclusivity

Is it the vampires' fault
That his aversion to crosses
Prevents him from exorcising his right to vote?
Is it the vampires' fault
That he can't do the school run
Come the Mourning of the Dawning?
Is it the vampires' fault
That rumours built on heresy
Mean employers won't give him the time of day?

Are we not all stakeholders?

It's not my fault
The Bitterns' Boom at dawn evidence of my calling

Archway Station

Smugness takes its breath when you push your hair behind your ears
With your oversized coffee cups and lipstick signatures
Along with outdoing bags with labels of vanity
Vocal intonation that questions your sincerity
Dignity is dimming as you search inside the bin
Picking up second-hand tabs that other mouths drew in
Competing with the courting pigeons pecking at your feet
Observe you from a distance our eyes prohibited to meet
Aspiration in a number-plate reedin not quite RI8HT
Aggressive overtaking returns to passive at the lights
Chasing in the woods and trees your rat race of a tail
Gate of the dream perceived, in time reality a GAOL
Arrogance in piety peeping over spectacles with solemnity
Excommunicated by sanctity
Doubting Thomas is whispering naggingly
Ensure you attend your church religiously

Terry Hans Christian

Comedian spotlight, anxiously perspiring
Audience iceberg, climate change defying
Heckler darkness, alcohol inspiring
Hyena not laughing prey he is eying

Survey the Serengeti and drift off to…...

A namesake northern town, a boxer lives there now
Clever to embrace a partner, canvas genius to paint
Thesaurus treacle secretes a face where pots chose to die
Whilst drinking a whiskey and brushing his thigh
Rivets of humour extracted from gritty shipyard monographs
Should have been making barrels instead of quantities of laughs……

Fighting fire with fire without an ember of a chance
There's beauty in violence nature in verbal eloquence
A plaintive submission with jugular exposed:
'Ok if you think you're so funny what is it that YOU do?'
Coup de grace incisively timed
'I'm a comedian what do YOU do?'

Summertrees Road

I rode my bike when I was ten
The pavement danger way back then
Avoiding dog poo in my line of sight
Now the shite peddle my road at night
I carried a blade when I was ten
From dawn till dusk clean and sheathed
My fishing line solely to cut
Innocence survived and thrived back then
I walked to school when I was ten
Cotton Parka green and red
The rain alone in soaking through
Hood not raised for ID to hide
I walked my road nostalgic for when I was ten
The street signs looked the same as then
The only devilment my young self to confide
Was playing Knick-knock on Kendal Drive

Mofff-Eaten Picasso

If Picasso had painted our bedroom wall blue
As opposed to me with help from you
The arty perusing chin rubbing crew
'What does it convey to you?'
I ask is the king putting his clothes on soon?
Are we indeed heeding the child in the room?
Well take your time with your navel gazing
Ruminate at your leisure to the claims I am laying
I talk for the many you elucidate for the few
I say the artist himself is a victim of you
Contemplating in the long shadowing light
With the heat of the day dissipating to night
Not only the season has fewer days left
The great man sat alone, silent, bereft
Imagery the cave language of humanity
The gift given I spoke with joyous alacrity
I'd prostituted for my celebrity
Can you sign your name for provenance clarity?
He mused on his muses
The sines of his life
Another line to draw
When he'd rather draw the line

The Medium

The sun rose but it didn't really
It doesn't rise for nobody: apparently
My head was scratchy from the night before
Non-compliant abstention from just one more
The patio of the hotel, quiet medicine for me
It's garden, natures' church for contemplation
Coffee and a smoke in isolation
Solitude to clear my fuzzy brain
I saw your approach in my periphery
But I didn't turn my head
My focus maintaining anonymity
Of all the chairs to choose in Casablanca!
Personal space invaded by your proximity
'I'm a medium' was your opening line
But on first glance of your outline
You definitely looked more like 'a small' to me
'I see dead people since I had a stroke'
I drew more deeply on my smoke
I'd been disturbed in more than one seance of the word
'Your fathers here with you he's looking out for you'
The mist was clearing quickly off the windscreen of my mind
*'William has his flat cap on and he's got Bobby with him
Everything is fine don't worry about a thing'*
I stubbed one out and rolled another one
'My wife will be wondering where I've gone '
With a final aside, that accompanied your uneasy gaited stride
'Tell your mother that your father's always by her side'

Schrödinger's dog

At 3.14am I awoke with diamond clarity
No flaws, hairs or atoms, horizon infinity to see
Eureka in a bed displacing Archie in a bath
Meads and ales inspired, ambrosial spectrograph
The laws of physics for the small and very large
Nonconforming relatively, cell celestial camouflage
Vexed the minds contained in planetary heads:
I'd wrapped them up in a parcel
Tied with a silky mathematical thread

Their hunting will be good and over
The Grail to Cox an amazing dream
Eddy and Nash would've stamped their approval
Nobel endeavour explosive, supernovas nakedly seen
Advancement is by a single step
Not by the synchronised March of Multitude
Not all would understand my reasoning:
The fog of consensus would mist the tangents and the signs
Comprehension slipping through the hourglass of their minds

Sunlight winked coy insight through the avenue of the trees
The congratutory sparrows chirping amidst the autumnal fallen leaves
My stride was purpose-full of self esteem
The cat by the store door looked knowingly at the man who had the cream
The elderly shop assistant pinged my coffee and salted crisps
'That's £3.25 but if you add any sandwich it's only £2.56'
Illogic ripped my logic, frayed my thread, doubts perturbed
'What if perfection needs imperfection?
Does it matter if it's dark with a trees' demise unheard?'
From the name-badge 'Albert' pinned obliquely
Upon his creased un-ironed shirt
Out of my eye-line as I was leaving
The semblance of a smirk

Mathew Street: A day in its life

Understated without the 't'
Milk without sugar that will do for me
Caustic curves not purely confined in porcelain
But passing by the window of Mr Flanagan
Doesn't rhyme in Queens but the scouser says it should
Best before date and sniff test failed
Dress sense inebriate, decorum jailed
Worst in class in an ashtray full of stubs
Was a socialising seal pup looking for a club
Searching for salvation in the dragging of a fag
Pursed lips from Speke: No danger of the theft of any breath
Complex in expression: Einstein at a loss:
Old bikes, chains dishevelled, homeless spokes unheard
Save for business acumen lying with dogs undeterred
Coat collecting statue having a lotta laughs
Plague of plaques on your houses!
Thoughtless selfies and photographs

Ah but the wit the charm the warmth in cold
It cuts to the bone sharpened and honed
Sarcasm maligned by those who think they know
But in reality conflation of arses and elbow
No more smoking upstairs on the bus
Fireman redundant waiting for a flood
He could still get a fry-up down Penny Lane
Safe in the knowledge that No Vegan Would
Jesus got the joke he was drinking at the bar
But the guys who stole his coat were also hot-wiring his car
Eleanor picked rice off the menu back then
But progress with process she'd find it hard to do again
Today I read the news Fentanyl rogue roaming interstate
But oh boy I've enough addiction already on my plate
Yesterday cast thinner shadows off the Caverns' weighting line
Regulators gutless, not in the physical sense
Let it be! Cane not Able triumphed in the fight
Kitchens in darkness except for foraging fridge-light

Shameful Tourist

Smallest nun I ever seen
Merging with the zebra on to San Agustin
Faiths' status and stature in decline
Inclination to a slippery slope
Charity first, last glimmer is hope
Tourists queuing on The Road to Domestos
Cleansing selfies at The Door of God
Indifferent fruit hanging on the lemon tree
Agnostic pigeons' peck and bob
It beggars' belief that a crutched wretch
Competes for crumbs from the churches' shilling
The bigger the door, the rustier the hinge
The flesh is weak and the spirit isn't willing
Pied Piper flag leads the silent on a requiem mass of drudgery
Facts ice cream melt, retention isn't necessary
He could say that the palace is made of Manchego cheese
It wouldn't raise an eyebrow be it in English or Cantonese

A Hill too far in Alcazaba
Another view to sea but I'd rather discuss it in a bar
Where a man stormed out, slow service in Lovento
He couldn't afford to wait another single momento
Street band wafting Sweet Caroline
Little kids' cute dancing midst the flow
Of people all shapes and sizes
Some wearing well, others dressing not Dancing in the Dark
A cymbal hat to pass inside the Gutierrez Bar

Serene magnificence in the sun-setting rouge
Roof balcony babble ignorant to the bliss
Man-toiled etched cliff-face backdrop lit
Art plays upon their wing with empathy
Of kestrels joyous in their calligraphy

Rhythm of a train moving down the track-tables of distain
Just a line not even a song, a repertoire of one
'Everything gonna be all right' sounds a little wrong
Smiling crocodile seeking contact of the eye
No woman no cry for cardboard people in doorway desolation
Pigeons make contingency for when the chairs are stacked against them
In Flamenco, the women earn their corn the blokes just say olé
Hope that when they divvy up they get the bigger slice of pay
Plaza San Francisco, bury me under the lemon tree
I'll leave a kitty in O'Connells for if you search to seek me

Lowry must have come here as a busman
From my perspective view of the distant breakwater
The wind waves through the bobble of little boats
One shape, one size, teacups in a storm
Along the promenade T-shirted bellies distort their words
Whilst all size and shape of dog wag their owner's tail

The cruise ship and the luxury yacht tied by tide in the dock
One beside one and the people two by two
All going to one and no one going to you
Predatory stillness you have to pass me by
To get to your little boxes piled so high
Oneupmanship, my box is stacked on top of you
I've got a balcony view on a floating zoo
Denominator of a human cargo ship
Entitlement common amongst the fodder
The lowest dine below the plimsoll line
Food chain stark, oligarch hierarch shark
No lights, no home, dark and silent no need to move
Functional in idleness dormancy to impress
The wealth with menace to know your place
Reflective waters of inequality
Relative to relative but no sense of family

Kate: The Rarest Egg

There are plenty of people who talk the talk
And pretend that they can walk the walk
Reality is they crawl the crawl
Worst in class they do fuck (nothing at) all
Then the people who can talk the talk
But who can also walk the walk
Depend on the people who just walk the walk
(Who don't see it necessary to talk the talk)
To listen to the talk whilst doing the walk
The substance of the plate is walking the walk
The garnish is the talking the talk
The stomach doesn't care for the talking
But the eye is never drawn to the walking
The most dutiful egg lets its walking do the talking
But the rarest egg does no talking or walking
They have no time for the crawling
But respect for the walking and talking
This egg makes all the difference
And should engender deference
The walkers and the talkers
Due diligence in their diffidence
A word in your shell-like to the crawling
With your exhaustive self-absorbing
Learn a lesson as you jog-on from the job….

The rarest egg just jogs the jog

Women: I salute you

The birth of a man is through a woman's pain
Memory regression as he grows himself a mane
The Matriarchal order of the big cats on the plain
Patriarchal influence lying sleeping in the shade
Rolling in from the Sunday boozer
'Is the dinner made?'
They say misogyny is in decline since Lucan hummed the song
'I value your opinion as long as you keep your pinny on'
Change is paraded in bright sunshine cast on a male folly on a hill
Casteing shadow betrays its unequal prominence
Intertwined linkage not one without the other
Say you'd like a little sister when you would prefer another brother
Adolf may have wound his neck in
Humanity stain erase
If his mother had raised a silent eyebrow
When she saw that moustache on his face

A Plenitude of platitudes
To soothe and to placate
But I tell you this:
In your candles' last flickering
Irrespective the rivulets your manly life has run
Your summation will have no relevance, no cause to analyse
Solely you will be seeking the succour of reassurance
Uniquely possessed in your own mothers' eyes

Ireland through the lens of a ten-year-olds eye

Spanish Point nostalgia for Blue Pool youth
No place for the fool only hardy fishermen
Pounding in its heartbeat, wilful in wildness
Armada destructive, magnetic, seductive
Burnt into the lens of a ten-year-olds eye
Edging pronation, ankles held tightness
Peeping non-blinking over edge into danger
Depth of the abyss, distance fruitless in gauging
Wind tearing in its harshness
Blurring in its searching
No light sight in darkness; only sound
Hooks buried in feathers in Tilley lamp flashing
Heroic silhouettes of manly men standing
Rods bending in straining, line vocal on winding
String of mackerel emerging from shadows;
Bouncing and gleaming, fresh in their shocking
Like a fish out of water, captured environ
Flapping and gasping for what it's not finding
Collective to perish but each one alone

Sip of a Guinness, moustache guilty witness
A guardians' nod to a boy's rite of passage
Sweetness to bitter tastebud transition
Stamp on the beat of a ten-year-olds heart
Relative of terrorist; sat stool-still, in his aura, at the bar:
Perception of danger in smoky-mirrored room
Uncles' protective cloak, imagery of a whisper he spoke
Sanctuary through the lens of an English boy's eye
Capped little old men, snow hair in it's peeping
Glacially moving, on gates they are leaning
Salutations in making with arm they are raising
Irregardless of strangers in cars passing by
Now rare in their numbers, endangered extinction
Habitat loss, social climbing in changing
Casualties to progress, cars now owners are washing
Rear-view mirror ghosts, nostalgia is sighing
For the lenses of a ten-year-olds eyes

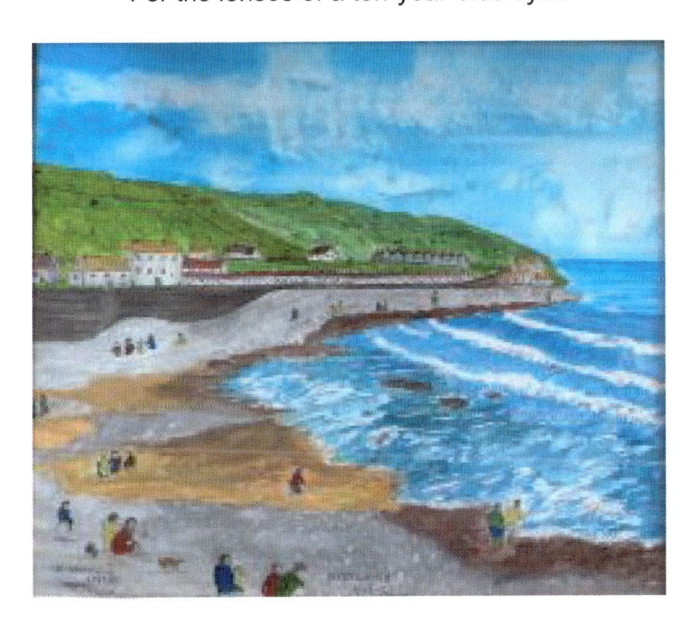

Jesus wept with Wolstenholme

It is what it is at the end of the day
Brexit means Brexit what does that convey?
Sound bites and slogans
Football phone-in parlance
Anodyne opinion, devoid of any substance
The countries finance built on sinking sand
An immoral code, a sleight of hand
Talking heads upon my screen don't listen to the song
They blindly follow Sat Nav though they know that route is wrong
The claptrap every Thursday is a distant memory
Thought Status Quo disbanded yet their strumming still goes on
I pay my tax an altruist, not alone in that you say
This blanket soothes complicit
Lying not in a doorway
Looking after Number one
Uncle Bob gave the direction
Yet the compass and its fibre
Fell through the trap door for the rats

Society gorged on by leeches spouting speeches
Dissonant voices serve lips paid
Floodlight failure, no spotlight cast in corners
Perfect night-game for the winger Alucard
The Christian teams of every cloth
Collecting souls instead of points
Could they look Jesus in the eye?
Or avert his gaze turn a guilty cheek
They kiss the badge each Sunday
REM plays every week
Play Solomon at number 10
Call on Morgan and O'Brien
Platforms to lift the fog of gloom
For we have it in our locker but we've lost the dressing room

Focus Early Doors 1999-2009.

I'll tell you of my lowest ebb: the ocean an imagination
The beach a swirl of sand, a scene from Mr Lean

Staying in a hotel, a swinging cat for company
Smoking in bed with an ashtray on my chest
Listening to the prelude of a loving symphony
The name Barry never bothered me before
But after so many affirmations now I'm not so sure
With the knock knock knocking they were bound to go to heaven
Though probably through the wall and not the door
I awoke in the morning perceived that I had nothing
And when there's nothing it is easy to choose
Showered with a dribble and a token of a soap
Dressed with Johnny Cash's greatest line
The agent spoke in condescension
When I enquired with good intention
The phone box didn't add good ambience
'It's an awful lot of money' his vowels were dripped in honey
But he agreed to send a quote: came second class

Jigsaw pieces have many shapes and faces
But all must fit content in their allocated places
The sum of the one to be less than the whole
A shine is fine on a shoe but it still needs a soul
Words I cannot dredge for thoughts fossilised
Adjectives abject for the meeting of love-burdened eyes
Money talks a lot but the heart dictates the sound
Substance is ethereal not merely earthly bound
The Importance of Being Ern
Esteem: Personification
It's a Wonderful Life

The work tap not a dribble but a resonant desultory drop
Reminiscent to the 70's and a camping toilet block
Credit card blanket limit stretched no matter which way it goes
Either under the chin or over sock-covered toes
Opinions like onions layers of potential to sting and tear
Formed and fermented beyond their first flush of youth
Memory has a bias not always sincere
And time is a thief that will hijack the truth
I've seen them come and I've seen them go
The good, the bad, the quick, the slow
A forest of faces many blurred to unknown
Some have fallen and some have grown
Characters many, some nondescript
(Shining lights) sociopathic personalities
Peddlers of lies (some the best of humanity)

It started off with uncle John
Could sell sand to the Arabs
And he proved he wasn't wrong
The bearded duo one didn't stay
The one that did had a powder-keg brain
Drove his convertible in the rain
His mate Mike was told he had a share
Came back from New Zealand to find it wasn't there
Shortest Arms and deepest pockets
Left soon after without making a profit

Another introduction came with cravat-dress-sense
Highly educated but his head was rather dense
Awkward and clumsy caused lots of things to break
Yet his voice evoked desistance of the offer of more cake
His Cupid arrow was sighted so many poles apart
Hair like Rapunzel, the bewitching Toxteth Tart
40 grit sandpaper yet he thought her grade was fine
The movie Shallow Hal followed closely down the line
Sadly unrequited - 'I do like John but just as a mate'
There weren't a lot of cheeses that could resist the urge to grate
Two stalwart Samson pillars joined to bear the strain
Did the work of many, reticent to complain
One suffered fools as likely as the desert accedes to snow
Had a long-term affair with Stella, loved his curry equally so
The other more complex, her brain a multitude of thoughts
Satisfying her intellect took her ship to several ports
Pushed the boundaries and made red the town
Glad she had a child and glad she settled down

Uncle John had been busy we needed to expand
We were driving crazy distance catching ferries to Ireland
Slim pickings: only women of a certain age
With romantic views of travel, scarves and nettle wine
Some had the view umbrellas were essential in the rain
'Best to get some drivers' Jane Austen did complain
Trained the era of the Chesney Twins and good old Kitty Clark
Joined us on the ferry and left when it disembarked

Her bloke was in the Royal Marines, she was undercover
She had no link to healthcare other than through her mother
The only knowledge she needed and her mind was very clear
Was that she inspired in many men a town in Cumbria
The south coast doc was smitten, wished me the best of luck
'No need to bring the machine next time as long as she turns up'
A glimmer of light from Belfast, likewise a troubled past
Red headed, pencil thin, belied the strength that lay within
She drove the roads of Ireland, no motorways back then
Exuded care: compassion dispensed with a loving spoon
A bird feeder in the garden of concern
Hopefully more than crumbs her reciprocal return

He was our inheritance, a caveat in a deal
A swarthy sweatbox of a man
No anti-perspirant could conceal
His mind was unionised, comfort blanket tightly wrapped
A working-class hero not prone to graft or rescue acts
Old-school tattoo in a snuff-box, time-faded swifter
Would homage a Haberdasher if he lost his little finger
Mr. Ron Seal, an appropriate pseudonym
Though what it said on the outside, rarely correlated within
The Three Musketeers arrived collectively as one
All in it together none was D'artagnon
The three whose names are reticent to the tongues of many men
Decent, self-effacing, grind-axe alien to them
Porhos' tales were Empire State, no one seemed to mind
A catalyst to think good thoughts: A Bon Vivant!
He loved intrigue, the cut and thrust
Generous in his manner, his allegiances not blind
His wife's IQ in empathy was in Mensa territory
Their kids' genetic soup, a worthy alchemy
Contrast with another rambler of the tongue
An invited guest who stayed much longer than he should
An anecdotal arsonist, emulsion optics verbalised
A void of self-awareness, a failure to comprehend
That by the beginning: You didn't want to hear the end

Athos wore a cloak of calm
Authority bestowed naturally not forced
His ambiance a saunter on a sunlit gladed path
Listened attentively and was generous with his laugh
He introduced another not cut of the same cloth
Who encroached on personal spaces, feigned not to realise
He lasted as long as the rope he made himself to hang
Amiable with menaces, a smile with disconnected eyes
Aramis hid his secret in less enlightened times
Straight talking opinions, 'poems should always rhyme!'
Drank copious Corona before their sales were to decline
Sickness come the morning, 'It must have been the lime'
A work-ethic that would shame most any fellow man
Drove the roads in demon-mode, speed cameras catch me if you can
But with the handbrake on, ignition off, engine yet to start
Silence: save for the beating of a gentle female heart

The first sociopath arrived on the scene
We were ripe for picking, an orchard very green
A self-made man it was professed who didn't need to work
No sense of shadows Mr Hyde in which for you to lurk
An altruistic soul going to turn the ship around
Bailiffs started knocking as the hull began to ground
A fantasist who preyed his trade who listened as he spoke
He'd phone arrange a weekend with Wrighty up The Smoke
He was a confidante to Zara, a problem-solving friend
'Say hello to Tindall, glad his knee is on the mend'
The year when the icy volcano chose to spew its ash
By the time it came to settle he had taken lots of cash
Deflection to the junior, office girl to much malign
But she dug up Bletchley Park, the sod was looking at serving time
The evidence was laid out like a Sunday birthday spread
But he gave back a little trifle and the copper shook his head
Escaped to his imagination, to the shadows Mr Hyde
His actions debated in his head and wholly justified

The office girl embraced the passing of the reign
QED: smallest head largest brain
Her epitome framed not cerebrally though
But as a pinhead trudging to work through the snow
The ship had found a captain bereft an ego cap
No alpha male syndrome to soothe and to content
Though chaos and ineptitude knew their race was run
Players Navy Cut smouldered in the ashtray of dissent
Walking the plank is easier with a swag full cul-de-sac
With the financial gun of influence now only loading blanks
The Doldrums navigated The Winds of Trade unfurl
Optimism a front runner with temptation to look back

Judgement

When the buttercups hang their heads
And the daisies have no chains to thread
When the hare of Keats in languish lies
Neath the tortured wings of dragonflies
When the birds protest in silent dawn
And cacophony shrouds the whales in mourn
When the beetle finds some pompous pride
And idles in his honest toil
Then tolls the bells of Hemingway

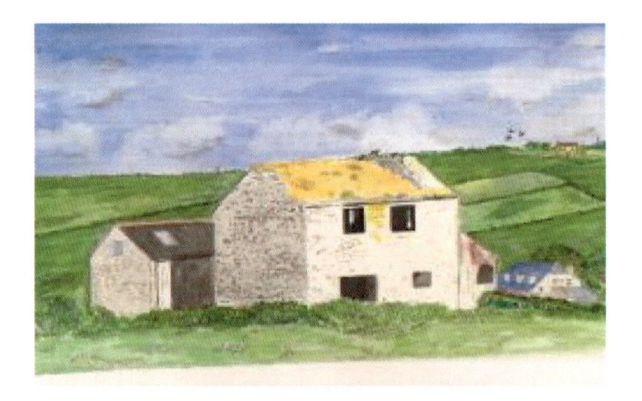

Euston to Lime Street

Stuart, the train manager, tannoy-asked all to notify
'If something doesn't look or seem quite right'
Don't ape the three wise monkeys
A vibrancy of vigilance, the perfect citizen would be

Now the arrows on the passage doors were troubling to me
From one side everything was fine, they pointed to the right
But suspiciously arousing, not at first I must confess
From the other side, not rightly but wrongly they pointed to the left
Was he aware of this discrepancy?
Was it my duty to query the direction?
Was my unease warranted and worthy to bring to his attention?

I heard his approach but forward facing in my perspective
I had to equate his personality by his approaching vocal intonation
I had my ticket ready, pensive in my hand
Was he amenable to my suggestion of a question?
Would he pacify my anxiety about the arrows on the door?
Or would he just stare blankly like others had so many times before?

I felt his presence, his aura, avoided 'eye to eye'
His efficiency suppressive to the raising
Of the bead-sweating issue on scrutiny displaying
Upon the furtive, furrowed brow of a fertile, febrile mind
My ticket presentation passed the mustard
But Cluedo thought-linked with Last Stand:
Duplicity in cowardice made the rhyme
Thus timidity ruled silence and with his insight oblivious to flaws
Stuart passed unperturbed through the arrows on the doors

Sentinel de la bodegas

The saged-aged sparrow sat in his dowdy brown
Tweeting his authority from beneath his sober frown
Slim pickings at the bakery the sol is going down
Best head across the bridge to the sunny side of town
There's a trail of potential breadcrumbs meandering my way
Then off to my cueva before the night consumes the day
Fledglings hear my heed whilst in your dandy-dapper-down
There's longevity in the shadows on the sombre side of town

Aladdin's Cave-Ron and Michael

The brightest lights create the deepest shade
Life cannot strive on soulless grey
To live your sense externalised
So brethren on your wave do ride

Seek succour from the Chopin breast
And frolic through the turning tide
Companionship does gently grasp
The butterfly within its palm

Embrace the embers of the past
Phoenix will flourish on your charm
Impressions fossilised in minds
Your genius of person-kind

Influential flow

I always thought of Mary when we reached the month of May
I only fought on Saturdays cos someone said it was ok
I ate fish solely on Friday, a decree from the Sea of Galilee
An aversion to every Monday, it was a weekly bath on Sunday
I only sent a card when I was told to think of mother
But Guy Fawkes is rolling in his barrel
Now that we're trick or treating one another
Turn the page, accept the age, no more vinyl to scratch and play
Nostalgia fights its corner but every dogma has its day

Therefore no need for a bigger boat, thank you very much
And I'm sorry but my name it is no longer Spartacus
Fear falls on deaf ears to the soundtrack of Jaws
It's no skin off mine mate to just blow off the doors
'God save the Queen' has sadly passed away
Written in the sand till the tide has had its say
Still send me a card but never on my birthday
White rabbits are for the month not only for the first day
Influence has aged, no more chiming of the clock
Fifteen minutes has wound up and ticked its last tock
Though a kingdom to choose from The Bards' river has run its course
Sadly standing on a balcony just looking for a horse
William must have written a zenith whilst wandering in the hills
But lonely remembered for his bunch of daffodils

Oban

Dog walkers exercise their faces
Ramblers synchronise their paces
Deference dominates the seen
Orca ferries steel across the classic postcard
Rain engorges the craggy backdrop green
No wafts of cigar in The Columba
No crumpled raincoat museum
Hotel signage alphabetical decline
Shrinking plates on which to dine
The Union Flag and Saltire
Flutter undecided side by side
Kids voices herd not scene
Babble on the seaweed breeze

Alex

Understatement is my norm
I was the same when you were born
Underestimation of my real emotion
Not solely embraced by the word spoken

Relief this time you made us wait
Like a three-pinted sweater for his blind date
Full time, extra time, penalty tension
Induces angst in the cross-section

Ahh.. but to see you lying so lovingly tired
A babe in arms, a tear inspired

A name for you and Tom to think
But like your grandads 'Big Kid'
To me she's 'Lily the Pink'

Redemptive Road

Sincerity to swiftly burn
Innocence to set aside
Pleasure to push its cyanide
And cast the net of wantonness
Upon the seas of loneliness
Head raised above the cavalcade
Of what is measured and what is staid:
Forgetful in its countenance
Dried fruit persists in penitence
And woe betide the pestilence
That rips the inner joyfulness
Of solitude and sanctuary
That covert all that's good to be
And factuates beyond the anonymity of pain:
Mundane sufferance ploughs the furrow
Brows of hills promise tomorrow
A maze of multitude
Escapades of mind subdued
When all is lost no wind no sail
No whiff of light on indigence fall
Sweet Father Time and Old Man flows
Will evade the confluence of poverty
Drain the depths of catacombs
And sow upon your stoical face
The seeds of spring in wrinkles frown
And desist the weeds of tumbledown

I.K.Brunel

A: Izzy's in hospital
B: Is he?
A: YES! Izzy
B: Is he alright? What's wrong with Izzy

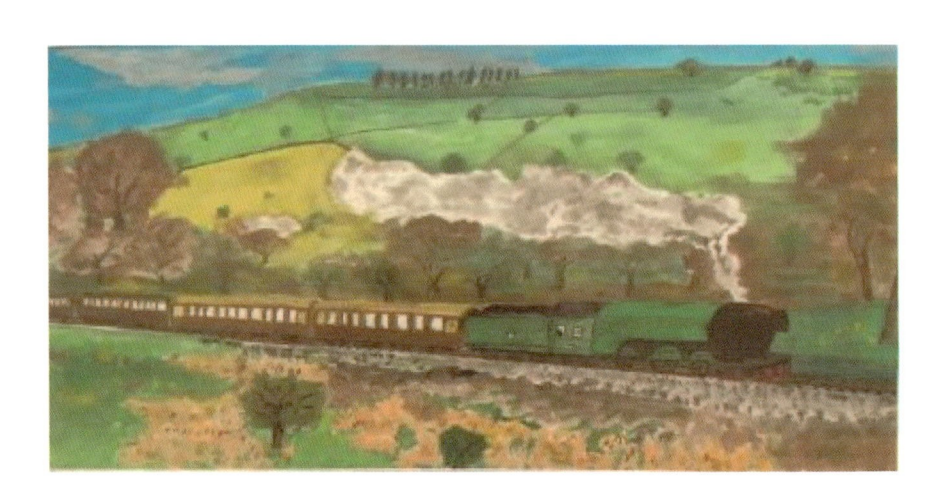

Good Job Alex B

I feel your stare of incredulity
Like I've just breezed in from the 19th century
Health and safety demands a hard hat
How you gonna wear one over that?
Just cos you're the main man
Just cos you wear it so well
What do you mean it's lucky?
What's all this 'Call me Izzy'
Special dispensation for whom the hat fits
Eccentricity touches genius and talent
Substance in portfolio, the conclusion to construe
Is that I will design and build the finest bridge for you

Commentators Glossary

The weight of expectations greater than when Pip was a lad
Lions on the shirt slumbering since black and white was all we had
They thought it was all over
But the wait persists till now
Bread and butter phrases through passages of play
Back beat and tempo the order of the day
No corridors of uncertainty in Hawkeye's in or out?
Cousin VAR does not draw a line under the element of doubt

Playing on his shoulder making runs across the line
Centre-half has him in his pocket, offside flagging all the time
Shirt sponsors groan that he didn't gamble on the cross
Class maybe forever but a yard of pace more of a loss
Drifts in and out of lethargy but he's got a goal in him
Comes alive inside the box thought it was his coffin knockin'
Comfortable on the ball playing out from the back
Looking for the killer ball not the simple pass
Good understanding on the overlap
When to go and when to hold
Beat the press, crowd vocally stirred
But quality lacking in the final third

Running in behind and arriving late into the box
Felt the contact and went down clutching at his shin
Penalty awarded but disgust shows no disguise
Keeper makes himself big as he tries to give the eyes
The Football Gods have their say but his technique was complicit
Tried to be too clever should have put his laces through it

He has it in his locker but the defence he won't unlock
A genius burning candles in the small hours of the clock
Arm around the shoulder or feel the hairdryer heat?
A Messiah can only take so much oiling of his feet

Pulling on his shirt when the game was getting stretched
Had no choice he was clean through, took one for the team
Put a shift in covered every blade of grass
He's got an engine box to box but lacks the sublime pass

Couldn't get the power as it was on his weaker side
Should have done better, at least make the keeper work
Couldn't sort his feet out as he'd left his right foot in
His corner didn't beat the first man standing on the post
No need for avocados, he's got the left-back on toast
Sitting back inviting pressure not the best form of defence
Didn't get his head up, lacking confidence
Took too many touches should have hit it on the volley
Should have pulled the trigger had his pocket pinched
Had more time than he thought composure rather lacking
Groans and whistles from the crowd, but he's got the managers' backing

Fans are getting restless voting with their feet
A stream of discontent reveals the colour of their seats
Directors maligned, sweeper itchy with his broom
No sympathy for the manager as he's lost the dressing room

It all makes sense to me

My mate Sid insists the world is really flat
The Pope is Christs' auntie, it's written on his hat
Lost in translation that Jesus professed to turn the cheek
God didn't need to rest after working through the week
Oswald got shot because he was a Cornish patsy
Namesake; an honourable Englishman
Not a fascistic, brown-shirted Nazi
Armstrong never made his step, flag flutter betrays the lie
Shadowy studio star he knew the eagle couldn't fly
Plain as the nose that Marilyn was Diana's biological mother
DNA would prove that they were the spit of one another
Lennon never imagined that the sky was all we had
Michael felt guilty about the feet he plagiarised
Paul was yesterday when he made that zebra crossing
Lucan shaved his moustache, lived unluckily alone
Elvis didn't die, it's spelt out on the gravestone
Goldilocks, a prima donna, bare facts of the matter
Charlie didn't make it, class-glass failed to shatter
Cinderella never lost her slipper it was all a princely ruse
Stitched up by the 'makers wife;
Naked abuse of elf benevolence;
No cloth forthcoming for the shoes

The Odd The Bad outweigh The Lovely

Vignettes of people intertwine like vines:

He was a low hanging apple pleasant to the eye
Look you straight in the face and tell you a lie
A limbo dancer who could manipulate
And stoop beneath the lowest moral bar
An ingratiate of ego, who gave less, professed more
A tempting shiny skin but rotten to the core
Dead Den would feel his pulse to check he was alive
He thought himself a maverick, a rock-and roll suicide
But his Hi-Viz and driving gloves betrayed the mirage
Minds mirror Mohican, real reflection, short back and sides
She was a breeze of life, no enigma in her smile
Oblivious in innocence her uniqueness to beguile
Pheromone caused attraction whether wanted or not
Far exceeding combination of trawler with honeypot
The pilot flying high till Icarus whispered in his ear
Self-imagery of James Bond helped push the envelope
Snake on the board took him back down to Basildon
Demotion, deflation, self-perception couldn't cope
Alpha male gorilla in the raging red mist
Anger management, failed triggers to desist
Fall from grace insulting, resulting in innocent face assaulting
A suave sophistocrat with crudity for fraud and theft
Diesel and jerry cans sleight of hand adept
Anxiety suppression in dishevelled hair and head
Victim evoking compassion that could never catch his eye
A lifetime spent unpicking the torment of his thread
Exhaustive, causative stress to amplify
A saint of patience would require a longer fuse
Sadness that his sadness equipped his subterfuge
The man that liked dogs was a terrier himself
Restraint of hands in pockets as eyes took items off the shelf
Could sing for his supper, could run the hard miles
Frenetic, peristaltic, heart of gold in atrial fibrillation
Glass half-full whether skies or legs be leaden
Character formed intact since jam butties at the age of seven

What's your s… threshold?

I'd rather eat my own
Than wipe a dog's tailed arse
If it didn't have a tail
I'd still rather eat my own
Not that I've got anything against dogs
I'd rather eat my own
Than McDonalds or Greggs
Fat kids with sausage rolls
Homage to The Biscuits
Not that I've got a profile to be smug and svelte about
I'd rather eat my own
Than at any other freely available fast-food outlet
Not that I've got anything against lawyers
I'd rather eat my own
Than look at cellulite on the high street
On badly advised legging wearers
Not that I've got anything against camels

I'd rather eat my own
Than take advise from a doctor
Who doesn't know his arse from elbow
Not that I've got anything against the band
I'd rather eat my own
Than listen to anyone with a cravat and braces
With a complimentary Plummy accent
Not that I've got anything against luncheon at dinnertime
I'd rather eat my own (or maybe not)
Than a single anchovy on a plate
I don't mind them disguised in a pizza
Not that I wouldn't prefer a snugly-tinned sardine
I'd rather eat my own
Than have a sense of humour
McIntyre and fruit poetry enough to bemuse me
Not that I've got anything against Scousers
I'd rather write my own
Than read some other shite being flushed out
Not that I've got anything against those;
Who try to make life rhyme with strive rather than strife

Parlezmeaninglesshotaireans

'We need to debate it in the house
You'll have to come back from Tuscany'
'Fine! Orate to your hearts' discontent
Vent your spleen have your say
And when you've sat back down I'll do it anyway
My gang is bigger than your gang
And they will all cow-tow the party line
Careers have been invested
My whips are cat o' nine
And if some waver, the consequence
To the back benches of Siberia
Figuratively not speaking because Coventry is nearer'
'I demand a public enquiry!'
'Fine! that's what we'll do
I'll get a saged-aged judge to forensically examine it for you'

The bleeding obvious tangle-tied in knotted words
Tree sacrifice for process, toothless and benign
Interest kicked a long way down the road
Redacted in the national dustbin
A rusty can to history consigned

Wind-up

I couldn't find Heinz beans in the Supermercado
Other brands were also not freely available
I had few words of lingo to explain and complain
Bald and naked toast not sufficient to satisfy
The desire for simplicity and familiarity;
But clear blue sky thinking came to the rescue of me
Inventive and adaptive in the face of adversity
Taken for granted like opposable thumbs
Ability outside the box, complexities to overcome
So I bought a jar of haricot and a tin of tomato sauce
I couldn't read the labels but the pictures helped of course
I mixed them in a saucepan with a smidgen of black pepper
Delia or Jamie couldn't have done it any better
My Numero Uno recipe wherever I may roam
Emotion feeds invention, there's no taste like home

Don Bradman

You have been my mathematical constant since I was a kid
Something Pi did not fulfil in its unending bid

6996/70 Magical!

I'd do the long division when I was nine and ten
Pencilling the numbers with a loving caress
Repeating the process fresh to the task
Reaffirming delight in a state of entrance
A Buddhist Mantra entwined in the beads
Dutifully passing through a nun's trembling hands
The greatest stat in the history of sport
Stated by many a booze-dimming bore
And it's true: no question no doubt
But the flesh on the bones of the fact
Makes its substance so much more than that

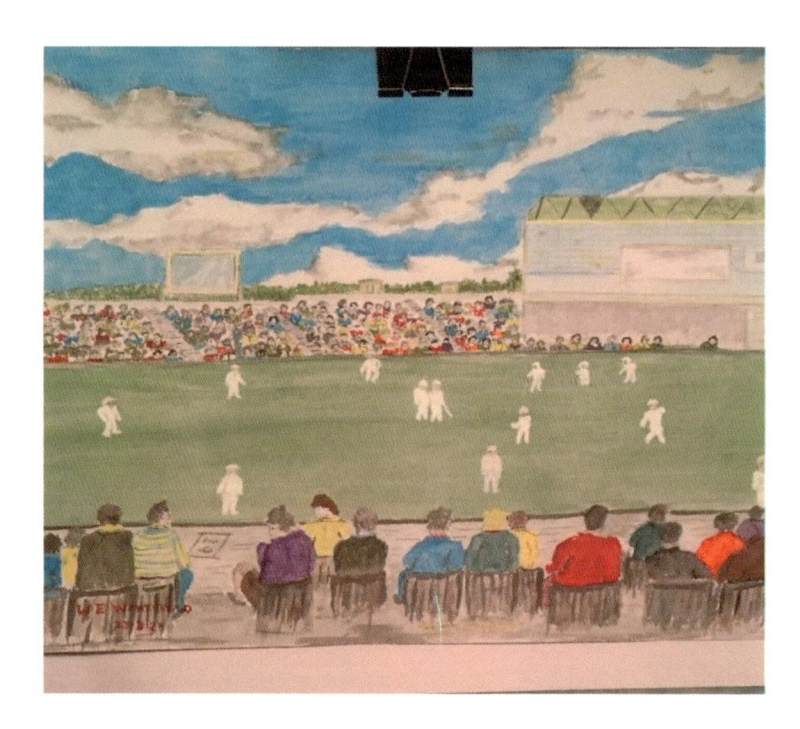

Era of The Gentlemen and Players
One knew ones place in the batting orders
Tone set by Grace, style and panache
He went against the grain of the establishment ash
Toured on his stage of 22 yards
No lofty signatures, no drives of finesse
Accumulation without any fuss
His fertile furrow the cause of bowlers' brows
His multiple run of runs called for a division of a plan
Raising questions of the body of the spirit of the line
Dishonour tarnished white flannels to win at any cost
Victory achieved; quest tainted; moral high ground lost
Red faces blustering in high places anger in the usually serene
The cause and effect of the little fellow in the baggy green
The 30's grew inclement clouding people's minds
Seeking umbrella reassurance wherever it be found
The mundane reliability that night would follow day
Sun returns the morning and that The Don was making hay

Music and sport sounds of my life
Mothers' rhythmic 50's fathers' bat on ball
The day the music died Buddy and his crickets
Interwoven synergy that Hollies took his wicket
Was it the moisture in the pitch or the moisture in the eyes?
His final exit through the wicker-gate doff-capped dignified
One four to the boundary the barrier to cross
But perfection cannot be exceeded without its meaning's loss

This calls for wisdom:
The epitome of man's striven metaphor
Numerically it is 99.94

Glasgow 1.30am

I saw you standing on the corner of George and Montrose
Your lines and curves illuminant
Stretching and submerging in perfection up the hill
Solid in your silence
I heard you through my eyes
I rolled and smoked in contemplation
Green and red incessant changing
No need or point a light for asking
Fat doldrums for faces no semblance of a spark
A quarrelled couple parting
Stormed off strident Montrose Hill
Left forlorn in the darkness
To cry or just to sigh?
Your beauty beholding but no eye in passing by

Granddaughter

Spent 48hrs in Idyll
Sunlit perfection
Attention
Alcoholic blast
But all was shaded
And perspective
For the moments of playing
With Lily on the grass

Rita Jacques

'Hannah and her sister' more compelling than the pluralised
Balls and fancy dresses mixing with the sanitised
Lords withdrawing to gamble on the shuffling of the pack
May have a pair of kings but they'd rather be holding Jacques
'Mirror Mirror on the wall
Am I Cinderella or is she?: Olive Oyl'
The Post Office scandal was way beyond the Horizon
Back then an early delivery proved rather more surprising
Born in the year of the Great Depression
Intrigue over her father, identity not confessing
First of eight the last came late
She had a child before her mother
Eve her little sister perplexed
That Terry was not her elder brother
Born into farming stock not shielded from reality
Cycle of life, the birth, the death, nasal scents of normality
Her Grandad had the longest arms proved useful calving week
Her mother white-faced collected alms no crimson for her cheek
She was christened in the family chapel of the noble Lord Brougham
Stirred up conversation birth connection silver spoon
Shank's pony relied upon too often for the size of isolation
Missing school she couldn't spell bad teacher taught her a lesson
Sat next to classmate Scarlett Fever hoping for infection
Wishing for some symptoms seeking toffee compensation

Your tales of Our Charles and Monty I will not plagiarise
Rogues are best described through sympathetic eyes
I've read your work you possess a warm enchanting style
So from head to page let it flow
It will be a well worth emptying
But it might take a while ……

My earliest memory is when I was about three and I lived on a farm in Cumberland with my one parent mother, grandparents, a great uncle, auntie and four uncles. I spent most of my time with my great uncle Isaac and this particular day I was with him in the hay barn and was sitting quite high up while he was putting some hay into a hand cart which had wheels and a shaft on it. All of a sudden he showed me some newly born kittens which he had accidently run over and flattened. This made me feel sick (cats usually find a nice place to give birth but were unlucky this time).
Just then I fell to the ground and knocked myself out then I started screaming and my uncle picked me up and put me into my mum's arms and she ran across the courtyard with me. My uncle used to put me to ride on the pigs back.
No memory for about two years.
Grandad, who had been the farm manager to Lord Brougham in Cumberland, bought his farm from young Lord Brougham, as he was called, as he had just inherited it from his father who had recently died unfortunately. The young Lord Brougham married an American actress by the name of Valerie French.
My grandparents went to the wedding which took place in London.
The young couple between them they squandered all of the inheritance.
Now everything is left in ruins after certain antiques were sold. It's a shame as I was christened in the private chapel which still stands but I am not sure of the condition it is in. I do hope to go and visit the chapel very soon.

Grandad lost his farm through fire. The haybarn had burnt down and it was
thought though not proven that a spark from the blacksmiths' chimney was the reason. This meant no fodder or warmth for the cattle so Grandad gave up as the insurance people didn't pay up and he was left in debt. It was no wonder as when the village people had no jobs my grandparents did all that they were able to do to help with food such as potatoes, turnips, bread (which my grandmother baked) and an egg for the unwell. My grandparents, mother, brother Charles (who I don't remember joining us on this earth) went into a little cottage for a few weeks. The cottage had one of those huge brick-built boilers in the kitchen (the type as the one on the farm) which had to be filled with water which was used for washing the clothes. One had to light a fire under it in order to get the water hot only on the farm we had our own washhouse and we had a huge mangle with big rollers which we used for wringing the clothes out. The washhouse on the farm was used by grandad to butcher and cut up sheep. Children were not allowed to watch this occasion.

The next month after arriving at the cottage my sister Val arrived during the night. I was six that week. When we had visitors, we children were not allowed to stay in the same room as them, let alone eat at the same table. We were given jam and bread and if it was fine we usually just sat on the doorstep hoping that the visitors would go soon.

My grandmother was so strict I was afraid of her in fact she showed no love at all only to Auntie Olive who looked after her during her long illness. When I was left alone with her especially when it was cold I hoped she would let me get into bed with her but she would not allow it.

Meanwhile grandad took employment as farm manager we were only separated for a few weeks and we all came to join the rest of the family on the new farm. I continued to go to the village school until the end of term and hated it. This meant getting taken there by horse and I was given bread and jam for my lunch and threatened by a very unkind teacher. If I had a day off because no-one was available to take me, she would be very threatening and bang her stick on the desk in front of me saying 'Your mother did not get up to get you to school on time, did she?'

Who has ever heard of anyone sleeping in while working on the farm? I felt nothing but misery.

At the age of six I helped grandad during lambing time in the way of holding the lantern during darkness when lambs were stuck inside their mother. Grandad having the longest arms was able to put his arm inside the sheep to get the lambs out Sometimes there would be three lambs and if it was very cold, as it is for early lambs, there would be brought inside the kitchen and put into baskets. This meant we had to feed them with a bottle which was magic for me only they grew so quickly and became very rough which meant that I was unable to feed them anymore. Sometimes we would have maybe five lambs a few kittens and a few puppies all in a basket by the fire and we were unable to get there ourselves in order to get warm.

We had gypsies stay on our farm from time to time and grandad was always courteous towards them and informing them that they were welcome to stay as long as they left everything as it was when they had arrived. Which most of them did as they knew that this was a place that they would be welcome again. One time grandad opened the huge Dutch barn doors for one family of gypsies and told them to push the caravan inside the barn as they had a baby and it was cold. He gave them milk and said to help themselves to potatoes and turnips but they took it literally as when he was coming up the street, he saw them selling the goods. Grandad could not stop laughing that's how he was and he always saw the funny side of life. As nothing so bad could ever happen to him as bad as losing two of his children in one week with flu and my mum was born in the middle of that week and grandad had rheumatic fever to contend with. In that same Dutch barn that I mentioned earlier we children used to climb up the wooden slats and tousle over and over until we landed on the hay; my cousin Anthony was the best at this.

In the orchard on our farm, we had a derelict cottage which was used as a hen house and us children used to play in it whilst the hens were out scratching and doing what hens do in the open. We would gather the eggs also goose, turkey and guinea fowl eggs from other nesting boxes. Unfortunately, this enticed rats and there were many and from time-to-time grandad would place a run in the cottage. He would tie a piece of string to the run and raise it a few inches and put chicken food in dishes inside the run then pull the other end of the string through the window. When a dozen or so rats had collected inside the run, eating the food, the string was loosened, and the run would drop thus trapping the rats. A terrier was placed inside the run and it worried the rats. I would call all the children to tell them of the forth coming event and with great excitement we would all look through the window to watch the horror. Now I find it hard to believe that children would find it so exciting.

At Christmas time we had orders for some of the poultry and grandad had to kill them. The geese seemed to know that there was something unpleasant going to happen to them. He would wring their necks then put a small knife through their heads each time he would say 'poor bxxxxxr' and hang them up to bleed in a bucket. I felt sick but still wanted to watch. My mum would do the plucking and my aunt would do the gutting of the poultry and would invariably have to gag and turn away for a rest. The feathers were used to make pillows and, in our case, feather beds which were lovely and warm to sleep on.

When we had thunder and lightning my grandmother would be terrified and sit under the stairs until it was over and she usually cried a bit. I've never seen anyone so afraid. When we lived on the farm one time the huge hen house blew down and my mother dragged the whole lot down to the back yard and as fuel was needed for the fire in order for my auntie to bake the bread. Without thinking that that it could be rebuilt my mother chopped it up and there it was huge planks sticking out of the fire. From time to time thy would go and push the plank into the fire until it was all burnt and then get another. It's the only time that I ever saw my grandad get cross.

At my new school I became very popular as the other kids wanted to play on the farm which they did as grandad was kind to all. We had classes come to visit to find out what farm life was like and they all enjoyed it. One day I got a bit carried away when some of the kids wanted to see what it was like to feed the hens so I gave them buckets of food and there we were shouting 'Chuck Chuck'. I had the worst telling off for using too much food. The horse's food was quite nice to eat and we all sampled it from time to time when no one was looking.

Harvest time was great fun during the lovely sunny days. Grandad would have his straw boater on everybody knew it was harvesting time because of that. We kids would be helping in our own way carrying the straw after it had been cut and it had to be made into stooks (a Scottish and northern term). If it rained during the night all the stooks had to be moved in order to get the damp from the bottom.

We found lots of baby fieldmice they were so sweet and we would make a nest for them. All the straw when it was very dry had to be carried to the barn where threshing began. It was put on conveyor belts where the grain was stripped from the heads thus leaving what we call hay. October was potato picking time and people even children during their school break had to be hired to gather the potatoes. It was back breaking work. The digger would dig the potatoes up and the rows were put into sections and two people to each section would gather the potatoes up. At the end of the day everyone was given as many potatoes as they could carry. Also, everyone had one good thing to look forward to lovely hot meals that my Auntie Olive made for them such as lambs head stew with loads of dumpling in it followed by a nice pudding, rice or tapioca.

My brother Charles who was supposed to share with me would never do his share and would mess about the farm and was just the same when we went to other farms to help out. On one farm the farmer helped me to do Charles' share and unbeknown to the farmer Charles would go and scrump the apples. Why? I do not know as we had dozens of apple trees of our own and he had the cheek to line up for his pay at the end of the day which he duly received.

When I was eleven, I started swimming lessons at the local baths. I should say the river Eamont which was covered in stones and broken glass as well as fish. Each Monday morning, we were walked there from school which was a mile and a half and we were tired before we got there. There was a row of wooden huts for one to change into your bathing costume but not enough for all. So, we had to take it in turns using the huts and leaving one's clothes in a bag, not very good on a wet morning. As far as the teachers, who were under cover themselves, it could have been brilliant sunshine.

The lessons began by us taking turns leaning over a bench doing the actions of swimming and when the teacher thought we were ready she would tell us all to stand in a row and we were told to jump in. If we didn't, we would be pushed in by her. Remember the stones and glass on the bottom? Invariably somebody would have a cut foot before the lesson was over. We would do breathing exercises and try to do the actions of swimming and a Mr Burrows, who used to help sometimes, would ask 'Does anyone think they are nearly off?'. My hand would go up and I was held under the tummy while Mr Burrows walked up and down with me, him wearing sandals and after two weeks he let me go and I was off swimming. What a brilliant feeling that as to achieve something. Then one day an inspector came and asked if someone could do fifty yards. Up went my hand again. I managed to do the fifty yards but she wanted sixty and I had the biggest struggle which took all my strength to manage it. A few weeks later I was presented with a certificate for that. How proud I was that is until I wanted to get it framed as that was not possible as my mother, who used to gamble, had written a bet on it. Then came the school gala. I was not good enough to take part? But no! There I was called out first and had to walk across this long plank over the river which was in full swell. I had no chance and came last and got washed over the weir. All I could smell was anti-septic as I was in the ambulance by this time and ready for off. All I could think of was the smell of the lovely roast chicken dinner that my aunt would have ready for me after walking home, no lifts in those days.

At school we had some children who were in a children's home and sometimes I thought they were lucky because they had parties and day's out and sometimes, they would go home to visit their mothers. My family never had time for things like that living on a farm. One day at school it was pretty cold and some of the children had no warm clothes so the teacher stood there and asked the class to ask their mothers if they would be able to give these children something warm to wear. I did feel so sorry for their embarrassment. True kindness came through when the children from poor houses had lovely warm clothes to wear. Some of the poor children had nits and periodically they had their heads shaved and had to wear those stupid poke bonnets until their hair had grown.

When I was seven and a half, I had been to hospital to have my tonsils out (in those days one's mum was not allowed to visit one) and when I returned to school a week later the class had learnt how to multiply four digits by four digits. Of course, I had not been shown how to do this and proceeded to work it out long ways in the margin and I was the only one with the correct answer. But I still got a battering from the teacher who must have known I was just home from hospital and had never been shown how to work the sum. What they would get today for such cruelty. I remember my young cousin Monty was beaten with a golf club across his back and he has still got faint marks of the beating to this day and grandad said not to complain because he might get worse for complaining which would usually happen. Four and a half years later the man who owned the farm died and the farm and everything had to be sold. It was such a sad time for us all, especially the men, they had to walk our favourite horses, cows and even our sheep dogs round the ring to be sold. Grandad disappeared to work for an old school friend of his for six months who was a sheep farmer, and lived at the foot of Saddleback, near Keswick. Grandad walked over Saddleback each day attending the sheep.

When grandad came home, he was happy to help his pension out by working for a potato merchant him knowing so much about potatoes. We rented a house down in the town which is now a British Legion Club which was such a change. We had a picture house and infant school opposite and we went twice a week which was great and on Saturday I'd have my sister Ann in my arms and holding Val's hand and we would get in for three pence. Cousin Monty when he was old enough would usually manage to sneak in and spend the entrance money on sweets. Sometimes sister Val would want more money to go to The Regent the second picture house which was situated at the other end of the town. As she had no money she would stand outside and put on a crying act and the next-door neighbour Mrs Kelso would ask her what the matter was and when Val told her that she had no money to go to the pictures Mrs Kelso would give it to her.

By this time, we were well into the second year of the war which did not affect us very much, only once we had a German bomber who had got lost and it dropped its bombs on a farmhouse about twelve miles away and killed the occupants.

When the German pilot was told it broke his heart. It was reported that what a kind man he was, it just goes to show that they were not all callous. Years later I was told by our German neighbour that if German soldiers did not do what was expected of them, they would be shot; just as our shell-shocked troops were in the first world war. Some Powers that Be would have a lot to answer for when they meet their maker. At school we used to pretend to be sheep and have to lie down in the field in case of an air raid, it was madness.

We all had gas masks and the one my little cousin had, being huge, as he had to lie in it. I wish that we had kept it.

Women has gas mask cases to go with their clothes. I remember my mother went to London for a few days to be with her then partner and stayed six weeks in spite of the bombings. The funny thing is she took my aunts gas mask because her case would not go with her coat and never thought about just changing cases and not fearing for their lives.

We had air raid warnings most evenings and at that time we had some Belgium gentlemen staying with us. We were obliged to take displaced people in at this time. During these air raid warnings, they would get all their belongings and bring them down and sit round the kitchen fire until the all clear went. We never bothered to get up that is until my cousin Anthony found out about the sweets and chocolate, they were willing to share. As we had sweet rationing, as most goods were at the time, needless to say we were there most nights and almost wishing for an air raid warning and we were very tired during school hours.

A little while later we had a Jewish lady named Rosenberg and her small son who came to stay with us. Eventually she managed to acquire a small one bedroomed property and her son stayed with us. On a Saturday I was asked to light her fire for some reason which was to do with her religion. I have no idea why.

After the war we had a Flight Lieutenant come to stay with us and he was learning the violin and eventually he wore one of the floor boards out. He had his war pension and took a little job in the Ribble Bus company and went walking on the fells which he loved as often as he could. He was an interesting person who told us stories about the war and he stayed with us till he died. I actually sat up with him the night before he died, on Pancake Tuesday, and at his funeral which my Aunt Olive attended everyone thought she was the next-of-kin as she did so much crying.

In my family I have four sisters and two brothers and there is twenty-seven years between myself and my youngest sibling and what I find so amazing is that we are all from the same mother but different fathers except for two of us. We all look alike even our cousins have a great likeness to ourselves that I did not know who was who at a family christening after not seeing that part of the family for a while. I said to one of the girls who was serving behind the bar.

'Does your dad drink mild?' and she promptly replied 'No that's Uncle Alan'.

We do have one or two graduates and a sister whom I thought was one day going to be a great writer and artist as she used to make up great stories. During the war she did a great sketch of the war effort with a man running and a penny behind him saying 'Make our pennies make Hitler run'. None of this happened and her only claim to fame was the she served The Duchess of Kent when she was visiting her barracks when she was in The WAAFS.

It's a pity no one was able to sew only Auntie Olive used to do her best. Bless her in repairing our torn clothes etc when we were small. I don't know how it started but I remember one time we had sewing needles stuck inside the wallpaper on the kitchen wall. Thinking back how funny it was when one wanted to sew a button on or repair a split seam hands would go feeling up the wall trying to find needle, lucky if it had a piece of cotton on it not caring what the colour was. With the help of my Uncle Alf who was my mother's cousins' husband I left home at eighteen and came to stay with my Aunt Hannah who was my grandmother's sister and had a small farm in Little Sutton. Unfortunately, accommodation was a bit tight as I was given a room with my Uncle Alf's mother Nana Knight and her daughter Lily who was great to me but very strict. I met my husband a year later and my Uncle Alf's sister-in-law Mary asked me after we had been engaged for a few months when we were getting married. I told her that we had no money and her answer was that I did not need money and told me that we could and live with her. We got married six weeks before my twenty first birthday because one got an Income Tax refund for that tax year. Except for a bit of hardship that most newly married couples have to go through, it was worth it.

It's getting better?

Good guys in white hats, bad guys in black
White guys the good guys, black guys the bad
Depiction of Jesus with blue eyes and blond hair
Polar bears and Snow White positively fare
It was the dutiful dove that succeeded in its search
The disappointing raven no olive branch to share

The rods and cones of little ones do not differentiate
Nurtured influence of thought, identity of feather
Snow blindness of my forebears history
Culture separates as well as brings together
Sussed out polarity not poverty of opportunity
Treating the symptoms and not the disease
But there's only so many slings and arrows to die for
Horses for causes becomes a scratchy needle metaphor
Tangible talent lends itself to cast a healthier pallor
Dichromacy kicks in beyond certain shades of pale
Black as your hat slinks to cool as a cat
A plethora of lives to choose
If you're playing for or singing the blues

The Red One overseeing Albaicín

Came to see the mysterious Al Hambra
Supposedly possesses the longest reddest beard
He wasn't available to see me, just like Willy Wonka
No sweaty golden ticket in my palm
'If you make an appointment he'll see you when he can
He has a massive following he's a very busy man
You could wait out in the grounds and gardens
It's very pleasant this time of year
Book yourself in at The Hotel America
If I have a cancellation I'll see you jump the queue'
So I had an americano con leche, just to fit in with the name
Enquired for availability, negative answer just the same
'Alhambra is a place, a palace not a bearded man!
Wondrous in its splendour as moorish as the greatest pleasure
I hope that lost in translation explains your estupidez'
Face reddening like a granada on hearing this bombshell
My coffee cup had lost its warmth as I held it in my hand
Behind the smallest serving hatch
Sniggering in a language I didn't understand
I'd been duped and led like an apprentice
Sent on an errand to fetch a long weight
Pride could not swallow my last drop of coffee
Throat dry of saliva I headed for the salida
Unnoticed nursing his coffee in the darkest recess of the room;
'The guy who lay the first stone indeed said to be a red head
Legend was his beard was ginger but that was long ago
Would now be such as wispy cloud above the mountain snow
You're naivety touches a more compelling humanic story
Than the fanciful façade of bricks and mortar
The tiles don't tell the tale but only bear the witness
Remnant relics of tatters of a golden Islamic age'

Columbus turned up looking for a sponsor ship
Armour prevalent but no ticks or stripes back in the day
He'd chanced his arm all Europe wide
Didn't care which flag he flew needed cash to sail his dream
1492 not only legend to the rhyme but also to religious crime
King of the hill but a fortress in isolation
Surrounded and submissive to a force of desecration
Tolerance veiled thinly a Trojan of a bride
A mosque into a Church means the end unjustified
The guardian of the door of the stained St Mary's
Gestured to doff-off my 'Robin Hoods Bay' cap
If he had the insight of the sentiment of the legend
He might have granted some special dispensation
Given that his Lord would have approved of his intention
A Purgatory of priests, fresh faith in their faces
On the steep cobbled rise to Albaicín up the hill
Blanket of doctrine priceless, serenity is cashless
Tab collars fitting tightly, their flock confess to pay the bill
Saw a novice nun with trainers on
Dangling her legs over at Casa La Debla
Taking divine inspiration from the view;
Same God, different teams, shifting sands of time
Possession of the keys dictating
Friday calling or church's chime
Had a cervesa Horno de Paquito listened to a Spanish guitar
It played there everyday but chord progression not gone far
Unlike the echoes of the cobbles changing
Rumbling Dylanesque wheels revolving
Pilgrimage of bucket lists, bizarre bazaars and Plaza bars
But my step was out of time with others on the climb
I'd come to see Al Hambra, of whom the whisper heard
Maintained that in his possession the longest reddest beard

Vienna means nothing to me but Rising Damp

When I began to write my poems
I did some research to see how it was done
Subscribed to poetry magazine and looked on Amazon
Discovery of a language I could not understand
View of a rainbow with just Richard of York
Decipher of hieroglyphics without Rosetta Stone
The discord not to understand
The working of an individual mind
Call a spade a spade, identity a shovel
A society intrinsic, witches' handshake, stirring hovel
Pull my woolly jumper on beyond my line of sight

How joyous to find a line!
As individual I dream and deem unique to me
What shapes to form and not alone in
This escapade, this bliss
Prevalence in it's antithesis
Alas I share no shelter in the fold
No cathartic ease to warmth
Ladders of understanding
Rungs of runes in abstentia
Confluence of forked tongue
The mediocrity of mind
Claustrophobic in its multitude
Genius in scarcity
A rambling riddle of ridicule
Cross word people torment for clues
Solution souly in the mind not on the page
Clarity a puddle a wellington boot abused
Scant merit in ruminations, reasoning obtuse

Stanlow

There was a goldmine on the edge of my town
It's now a shell of itself, ghosts haunt its rusty frown
No nuggets or holes it was much more refined
Generations turned a blind eye to the skyline it maligned
Constant flame, eternal zippo light
Whatever the weather it burnt brightly at night
Boys of the black stuff pockets of cash
Money for old rope from broom to boardroom cats
Nepotism strode nakedly in any recruitment drive
Not the sharpest in the box but he has a handicap of five
No secret handshake but a smug look around the eye
Alumni of nicknames ending in the letter'Y'
Hotel California in the Cheshire countryside
Serve your time, no attempt to misconceive
Cheque out with your pension pot or die before you leave

The Suffix on Sufferance

I am -ism that acts like a prism
Dealing in separation of thought instead of light
A Kaleidoscope of change I've seen
Throughout the lexicon of my working life
Golden boy -esque although in fairness has grotesque
Basques in the genii of Bradman and Chaplin
Whereas the guests I bring to the party
Have a paucity of charm
Namely the cronyism of Thatcher and McCarthy
I have no objection when it comes to sex and race
And I take my part seriously in the setting of the tone
But in regard to social and ideal, my intonation flows uneasy
Ditto to the denigration of the altruism of Marx
Impartiality I embrace like the monarch of the realm
Due candour has been seen to serve me well
But like Canute I brace against the tide of cynicism
Its rise and rise, no cause for optimism
I accept that realism is the butter on my bread
That my punctuation holds a certain gravitas
But the spectrum that negates can be cutting and unkind
Though the positive correlation that you will definitely find
Is that amongst the greatest innovators
They all had autism on their mind

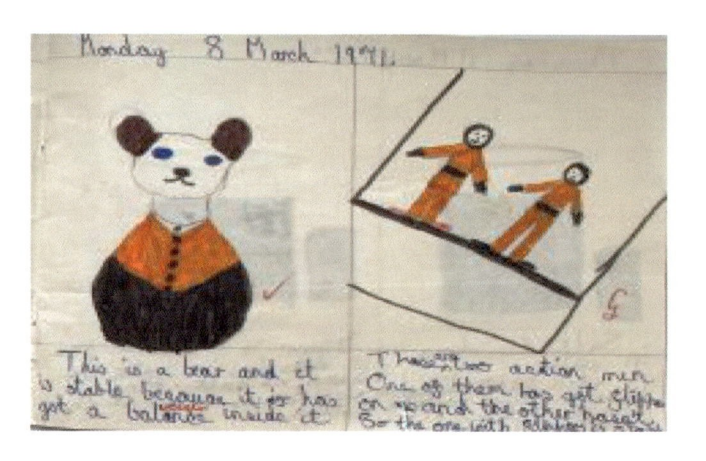

Farantóireachta carraig

My social mobility stalled right there
When I chopped off the end of the Camembert
Rose tinted sunset horizons to fade
Curtailed by abuse of that cultured of blade

Eyebrows angled on superficial faces
Linen topped tables holding airs and graces
Waspish glances stinging my self-conscious
Hole and swallow, pariah obnoxious

The lightest of touch on my shoulder perceived
An elegant clasp of my wrist interweaved
Like a betrothed pair their first slice of the cake
Along a parallel line our mark we did make

'La plus geniale des hôtesses'
Stood stately, satin and pearl
A wink and a nod, equal measure
'T'inquites pas!
I'm a Rock Ferry girl'

The Human Nature of Birds

Extremity of the albatross, bravado of the sparrow
Thermal ease of the eagle, aloofness of the owl
Reliance of the robin, Red Arrows of the hawk
Poverty of the pigeon, scarcity of the lark
Jekyll of the magpie, Hyde of the jay
Twilight of the starling, malign of the crow
Last orders of the nightjar, overcoat of the rook
Privilege of the peacock, serenity of the swan
Knave of a kestrel, vampire of the bittern
Judgement of the blackcap, anxiety of the chicken
Spelling of the ptarmigan ditto capercaillie
Dambuster of the cormorant, Munch of the shrike
Diligence of the penguin, mystique of the merlin
Train of the mallard, party of the bunting
Blatancy of the blackbird, façade of the cuckoo
Fish for the Kittiwake and chips for the Herring Gull

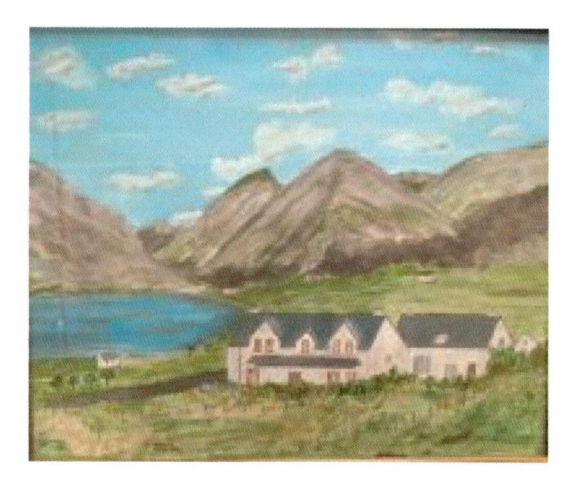

Arrogance

Climate change is all the rage
Fires and floods tsunami waves
The Earth don't even blink an eye
Self-indulgent causation, veracity to amplify
Mere seconds on a timeless clock
Ability to think and ponder
Breeds arrogance and soul indulgence
Gods imagery, a mirage to comfort
The desolation of the unknown fortune
Simplicity to complicate and contemplate
The reality of nonentity
Faith flickers in its fantasy
Scatters its ashes in its purgatory
Straws beyond the clutch of best laid plans

The lost cities of the Golden Arches
Will perplex and puzzle the next
Places of worship they may surmise
Gods of burgers and servants of fries
Amongst the tangled undergrowth
Cathedrals and Mosques intertwined with vines
Common ground found, nature not particular
In its distinction, extinction not its concern
Titanium and silicon telling on decay
Life in a lifetime succinct in its duration
No bones of picked contention
Puzzle of fate: two plus two is four

<u>Nigel: A cut above</u>

An oasis in anonymous
Your craft possessed is all but lost
The giving of the twinkling eye
Far exceeds hello goodbye
Your counter is no boundary
Your apron hides no strings from me
I prefer to pay the extra pound
To hear the joyful dulcet sound
Of a master of the spoken word
Sincere tonations to the heard
So for the succulence of the chop
And for the ambient fragrance of your shop
Though no credit given to purchases made
You deserve a great deal for the giving you've gave

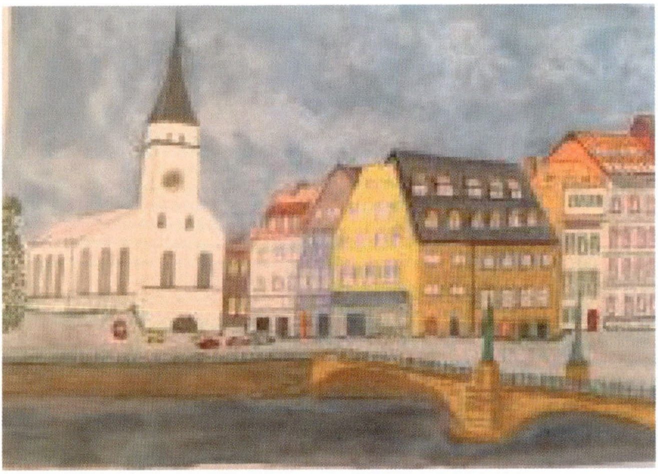

William Ernest

'They were collecting for Africa when I was a lad!'
Subtle sardonics from my old dad
Born when the scent of war wafted the air
An absence of father, an urchin, a boy
The eating of candles, the sucking of coal
Frozen glass windows, attic room cold
Leicester Grove and Leicester Place
Woodhouse Moor and Blackman Lane
Echoes of childhood, delights in the pain
Bananas and underpants late to appear
Organ tuning denied; Jimmy Morris the scamp
National service, the pseudonym 'Butch'
Taffy the boxer and RAF camps
'Rock around the Clock' merged with 'Peggy Sue'
'True Love Ways' arrived on the 'Rockabill'
Nora and Butch John and Marie
Mick and Bridgie couplets
Family stability
Milk floats and railways, tarmac and footings
Car plant, steelworks, bleary morning haulage
'Fiddler on the bread?'
Dough for the mortgage

Proud as a fledgling when he learnt how to fly
Puffed up his plumage, stood six feet high
In watches and clocks he was to formally train
A magpie of shimmer in his garage remains
His view of the world was through proud English eyes
Of Nelson and Churchill and Dog-fighting skies
Yet through marriage and friendship Ireland was kin
Butch was his name, they thought highly of him
He had a bag full of praise for all the grandkids he saw
His insight with hindsight annoyingly sound
His charm was imbued in the art he produced
A tangle of talents. A warm hearted man.
He surprised to the end, content to his fate
As he talked of the angels secure in his plans
They lay there unnoticed hidden in sight
My father's possession of the most beautiful hands

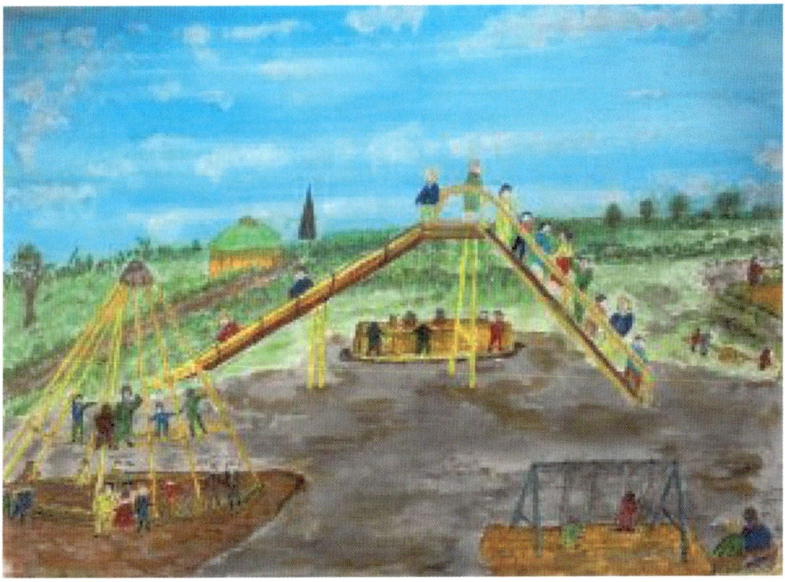

A poetic journey starts with a single phrase
Grows with growing pains across an empty page
In time becomes a pamphlet progression to a paperback
As a Cancerian: I always aspired to have a Hardback

Cheers

Opinions like onions layers of potential to sting and tear

r@slothpigrizia.co.uk

Illustrated by W.E.Wakefield

Printed in Dunstable, United Kingdom